Aphrodite Fever Dream

Poems & A Short Story

Katie Ness

Copyright © Katie Ness 2023
Editor: Isabelle Call
Book Designer: Anna Berzovan

All rights reserved. This book (or any portion thereof) may not be reproduced in any manner without written permission from the author except in the context of reviews.

First published by *The Undressed Society Publishing* 2023
www.theundressedsociety.com/
1st Edition

Book Cover Photograph © Alice Alinari via Unsplash
Bio Photograph © Keith Craig Goodall

Katie is the embodiment of Arachne herself, intrinsically weaving together her experiences, her spirit, and carefully crafted phrases to create the most beautiful poetry.
Isabelle Call, Editor & Publisher
of Poetry Undressed

'Katie's poetry is visual feast and stirring read'
Hecate Magazine

'Katie has this delightful way of seemingly painting with words, such a kaleidoscope of textures, layers and emotions'.
Claire Walker, arts reviewer and essayist
on Corridor 8

'Katie's writing resonates like an orchestra, each of her words vibrating with a different frequency on the spectrum of human emotions.'
Soumyajeet, Editor of Rebelle Society

Katie has a beautiful way of combining words in poems that flow naturally and make you feel like you're going on a journey with her.'
Emily King, Founder and Editor,
The C Word Mag

The great and amorous sky curved over the earth, and lay upon her as a pure lover. The rain, the humid flux descending from heaven for both man and animal, for both thick and strong, germinated the wheat, swelled the furrows with fecund mud and brought forth the buds in the orchards. And it is I who empowered these moist espousals, I the great Aphrodite.

Aeschylus, The Danaides 463 BC

Content

The Oracle (For my Beloved)

The Snow Priestess with the Poppy Heart
(For Sarah)

The Sky of my Body

Luna Moth

December Dawn

Honeysuckle Summers

The Priestess of Perdition (For Wendy)

Sura's Fox

Insignificant

When the Roses pulled the House down

The Memory of Aphrodite (for Despina)

Beautiful Metamorphosis

Persephone's Descent

Clear, Bright (For Claire)

A Quiet Crushing

A Letter to My Marigold

The Priestess of Black Pool

Stranger Baby

Hekate! I keep your secrets well

I will be waiting for you in my palace of grace
(For my beloved)

A Hymn of Love to the Earth

Rebecca's Requiescat: I dream that you forgive me and my body turns to water (Short Story)

The Oracle

She is a whirlpool.
With a heart of misty merrows.
He is a simple man. Of the earth and humble.
Enraptured, but he does not understand.
Her stories are tornado tongued and tidal
Her stories are about a jungle and kelpies.
No, her stories are about magpies in the magnolia tree,
Cypriot coffee and saltwater eyelashes. A shaman
   in a waterfall.
A pregnant woman casting spells. Coconuts on the sands
   with a hummingbird.
Mermaids, pigeons and fruit salads. Citrine tempests,
   dog walkers and a pirate.
She talks like a fever dream and he's trying to understand,
But she is a cyclone. Her mouth claps like thunder, eyes
   lightening bright.
Her heart is like a storm in an atom, blood flooding
   through her body,
She is deep in the moment. Deep in her pomegranate
   reverie.
He is patient with arms stretching from a sunset
   skyline smile.
Stretching out with a cherry tree embrace.
Her body melts in his chest; rooted.
Obsidian curls cascade at his elbows in willowy rivers.

She is complicated like this. She is a concoction of wild
    flower thoughts,
Of hazy days and sun kissed shoulders and
    Aphrodite poetry.
He is with her, silent, enamoured and waiting.
Finally the story rushes from her lips like a spirit and rises
    with the moon.
They are standing ankle deep in the ridges of the
    dreaming pools.
And now he understands.
He is a Canary island lullaby with earthy scouse devotion.
He wants to hold her. To cherish her.
He is the size of an oak. He is robust love.
She is dandelion seeds released in the wind,
He is the branch gently grasping her as she takes flight.
All the while, the ocean watches them with its mouths
    wide open, witnessing,
As they kiss, pouring their love out into the world like a
    tropical storm,
Loving each other like two turtle doves.
Passersby stop and stare,
Glancing sideways, elbows propped,
wanting, yearning,
for pieces of that sweetness,
Famished; Like crows.

The Snow Priestess with the Poppy Heart

Sex is a storm and I am the fire-dipped butterfly,
I am all of the irregular passions.
A blazing queen on my crystal throne like a scalding star
　in the frozen, polar night.
Sovereign arctic leopard, snow stalking in the shriek
　of frost.
Foxes glide at my feet like a sea of rubies,
Roaming with the moon on my face and the wilderness
　on my breath.

Offerings of sinful pomegranate kisses,
my capricious mouth; a single radiant poppy,
smiling curses that strike like scorched ice.
Blushing lips at odds with the sharpness of my teeth.

Steel blue eyes, intoxicate and harness deep waves of the
　ancient Siberian seas,
at once malicious and caressing.

In each bottle of nail varnish a banshee wails,
Like a thunder clap,
Like the wrath of the vestal virgins,

Men think themselves beasts but they are merely lambs,
begging to be sucked dry;

Like the pulp of beetles devoured by the scorpion,
Slaughtered hearts on altar slabs to be pickled in jars
  next to the vegan soufflé.

Kneel at my feet, I am your fate.
I bear my breasts and your secrets are unleashed under
  the sheets,
Softly caressing the ruins of another morning soul,
Panting like cherishing dogs, warm tender animals;
A savage satisfaction.

I dream in silk and scarlet-stained Pythian promise,
A Rendezvous of whips and shackles and flesh magic,
Purse my Brigid lips at the pleasure of fruit hidden
  behind the veil.
Peach-tease; paradise stems, preach the scriptures of Eden.

Dripping wine and curses down my ankles,
A sorcery of fervent hands, of heady elysium and
  siren psalms,
Of the despotic seas. I am your grail!
Both harlot and honey, fair is foul? Foul of mouth,
  fair of heart.

Velociraptor woman, clever girl- I am a cunning cunt!
Lap it up! Get it up, and I'll hop on top, I'll wail
  and screech!

Play you like songs of Sappho,
Like a La Belle Dame Sans Merci Nympho.

Sex is my armour and I am the paradoxical panther,
I am all of the tempestuous love!
Torn between leaving scratch marks on your chest,
Or purring to the shores of your heartbeat.

But I keep snowdrops on my skin,
Delicate yet tenacious in the glacial breath of Cailleach
Suns and skies, seas and swords,

No one knows my swift heart, Secrets kept in stone
  and parchment
Mask-Callus, but my heart is bluebell breakable.

Expectant hands are the gateway to paradise,
I am an everlasting brutal rose, I want your blood for love,
Before the dawn, I'll rush away with the hush of the
  vixen's call.
I shall swallow you all like snow consuming mountains!

The Sky of My Body

For the waters and the mud,
For the moon and the stars,
As the dove dances in the breeze;
And as the trees speak the language of eternity.

As the morning makes love to the night,
A garden climbs ardently from my chest;
And I yearn for you to free the wilderness buried
   in my heart.

And the birds of my soul escape the cage.
The wildflower grows from my lips.
I love you like the magnolia tree loves the Spring.
I kiss you like the river kisses the sea.

I merge with you the way time makes love to the seasons.
My heart beats with yours the way birds soar across
   the sky
and the bee hums in the meadow
and I am at peace in your arms like the daffodil held
   by the earth.

I want to taste the summer rain of your body,
Like the river flowing from the mountains.

Your hands like rain pour into the sky of my body,
The warmest taste of your tongue,
The soft sea of your salt,
The secrets of your stoic heart,
The wild plum of your blood,
And I am writhing like a kestrel aloft wistful waters.

Your arms like pines reach up to the heavens of my soul,
The feral fragrance of your skin,
The private delight in your moonlit eyes,
The primordial sun in your bones,
The undressing of my throbbing heart,
And I am unravelling into a thousand sensual stars.

It is always with love. It is always for love.
I am waiting for you darling, waiting for the words.
Just say it and nothing will stand in my way.

Luna Moth

The sinister grains of the Luna Moth
Beat softly, insipidly.
A slow dissolve of animated dust.
Papery wings stalk the moon like thirsty birds.
I was your clear pool,
In the slick liquid of lapis,
I am the beauty of ever after.
I am the flash of the heron and the hare.
Did you ever imagine that my love for you
Could radiate roses?
So deep, so red.
The petals fall like shrapnel,
I dream that you think of me,
And my body turns into water,
Opalescent, cool and pure.
You are the beauty of unknown territory.
You are the bite of the spider and the snake.
In these crushed-cherry hours,
Blue secrets drowned in the darling fire.
There is a black mirror between us,
My body shudders for release.

December Dawn

The snow melts faster than you can catch it,
Metamorphic clouds trickle like breathing rain,
The sky blessed me with the turquoise imagination
   of god.
Ducks laugh together like a cackle of babushkas,
Settling the rage of winter.
Dark waters crystallise antique crisp leaves,
Soldier trees stand, still and silent to honour the harsh
   beauty of frost.
They feel the silence of the ice.
Icicles cling to the blades of grass like a lost
   lover returned,
You interrupt my pretty reverie with a warm smile.
Time has frozen yet life will soon awaken from its
   persephone slumber.
Everything is at a crossroads in this world,
And waiting to begin again.

Honeysuckle Summers

Standing in the back garden, she sees the rose free spirits; Those beautiful creatures have bloomed twice this summer. Their aura; delicate yet raging, drifts upwards like heat waves at dusk. The entire garden echoes with the chirps of bees and crickets, Each insect emits little pink sparks of love that flicker with their wings. A message of reverence to the roses. The mauve coloured air weaves through the sweet grass and the lemon balm as the young woman sits barefoot, with her hand on the earth; begins to grow a honeysuckle from her wrists that stretches across the wall of the house like a flying fish leaping out of water.

As the sun sets, she paints moons to hang on the willow tree, Its branches curve over the fence and onto the main road. Fleetwood Mac's 'Dreams' floats through the air like a cloud of fever dream nostalgia. *"Now here you go again, you say, you want your freedom…"* Passers by would stop and stare at the moons orbiting in the tree and remember a time when they were children, a time when they believed in magic and a thousand other things they'd long forgotten. The neighbours soon whispered that if you kiss the one you love under the roses, they will be yours forever. Adolescents with arduous hearts would be caught sneaking their lovers over the fence at midnight, for a moment of passion as the petals rained over their lips to bind the spell. The floating moons watched over them in the heady breath of late summer's night.

The Priestess of Perdition

Under the Texan heatwave, Fig trees bear fruit like
plump breasts in the fever dream sky, Next to the evening
primrose and jasmine climbing ardently up the trellis-
like veils of snow, Raining petals; tiny angels falling from
grace into the deathly mouths of the bat-orchids. And
the burgundy roses sway on a breezy thread, tickling the
deckchairs. Teasing the arms to touch them. Everything
is burnt here, even the native accent sounds over-heated;
Slow cooked; Strange to me. But I desire water. Tropic
of Pisces born of Californian seas. Skin, moon-bright
carved by petroglyphs of Sa Pa mountains, retro tattoos,
and silverfish runes of Saigon. My face, like a Vietnamese
oracle, inherited features from an ancestor long ago. I
feel her live on in me, a silky iris-eyed tigress, stalking
customers from her floating palace by the Mekong River.
Forecasting your fate from Pho soup and jade chopsticks.
I'm a Moody sea-salt naga with the soul of a river, I am
caught between two worlds that I daydream of often,
standing in denim shorts and a black, velvet choker by the
pool, stoically smoking a cigar, You don't understand me,
you see; I'm a satiated siren with runaway spirits, painting
wicked women on canvas. A red cardinal perches by my
kitchen window as I cook the stew, peeping at the storm
in my mouth and the cirrus in my eyes. And I wait for my
Odysseus to voyage home and rock the boat.

Those listless tarot toying days pacify my smouldering sulkiness, Scrying memories like a desert wasp navigating grains of sand upon the open road, as the pretty heart-shaped spiders hang from the cactus-like mother-of-pearl. The pool anoints my body, Whilst Lana del Rey's *"Blue Jeans"* floats through the air like smoke rising from a cauldron. Reminding me of the first time I met my cryptic cowboy lover, at Peggy Sue's Diner on the road to South Carolina. Two lovers in a rental car together, colliding in a rated 4 Tornado on Myrtle beach, As rain cloaked the windscreen like a sea god's beard. And so I praise the dark clouds growling wild like a black cat peeking over the rooftop; it reminds me of that kismet day. That day of rain kissed promises, milkshakes, and magic….

The smell of incense and fermented fruit coil through the doorways and into the yellow diamond sky, I cast secret spells that snake through my skin and slither between my legs, Sigils hidden beneath tattoos that summon the soft-light memories and protect me from Ophelia dreams when I sleep. The neighbours know I am a witch, but I am too coy to care. Down the dirt road, I am woad and womb and worship. Seeking sun-fruits and moon moths for soothing hearts broken. I've cut my nails short to avoid scraping your palms like scratch cards to foretell your future. But I can pluck premonitions from the

paintings I made at 3 am on my front porch and whisk up a love spell in your coffee. Darlin, you may think me a pretty shy flower but I'm a Belladonna woman with a hex and a box of matches in my lingerie. The toad stares into the drizzle with two cold obsidian eyes and vibrates underneath the plant pot whilst the hedges unravel in the yard like ribbons. Words drip from my lips like water over the kitchen sink; croaking curses and promises into passiflora pie. The capricious scarlet-girl ghosts send shivers through the beams of the house like a murder of crows.

The prophecy is not my fault, It's not my fault! I say to the dead bee. Her tiny heart breaks for me as I place her on the altar. I appear delicate; curled as a rose, yet my cat's eyes shine pure, black stone Jet; all at once caressing and stoic during talks of poetry, sex, and sunsets. My twin chose the family life, I chose the untamed life of quiet aches, incantations, and invoking Nephthys. Every night I used to pray I'd find my people. But the black cat holds more interest to me. Swooping in on her predictable prey like a sybil throwing bones. I was no longer the victim. The phantoms that haunt me understand me better anyway;

Đất, Lửa, Gió, Nước, Mặt trăng và Thần. Mang lại cho tôi bình yên

I yearn to drift away to where Hằng Ngã and Địa Mẫu
and the rest of the everlasting daemons entertain dreadful
divinity. I have lived many years of wild rovings on
the road to nowhere with saucy secrets secured in my
petagram patched back pocket.

But I am bewitchingly blue jeans free.

Đất, Lửa, Gió, Nước, Mặt trăng và Thần. Mang lại cho tôi bình yên -Earth, Fire, Wind, Water, Moon and Spirit. Bring me Peace.
*Hằng Ngã is the Vietnamese goddess of the moon
*Địa Mẫu is the Vietnamese goddess of the earth and underworld

Sura's Fox

At first there was ambivalence,
Witnessing the elegance of rain clouds
and pink chested pigeons.

Light turns dove grey.
Within the trees there is a song,
It lulls the first layers of sky,
Awakens the muddied dandelions,
Lilacs shouting tender leaves.

A rush of red fury in a soft leap,
Sharpe libertine velvet,
I was not looking for her.

But her flame smothered the bracken,
This tender fire and exploding hearts.
She must have wanted me to feel it,
To crave the effervescent, cunning beauty,
Artful gentleness, bloodied cutting voice.

She sang of the elements,
That pretty vicious face!
My scarlet, fanged angel.

Insignificant

Black eyes, mirror distorted.
I could write sonnets and poems about those eyes,
Just a concept,
I am just *your* concept,
A fucking necessity!
Bitter, it's bitter.
The ashen taste of you in my heart.

When the Roses pulled the House down

Kī shan i Romani, Adoi san' i chov'hani

The house smells like honey, crickets and sweet-dark treacle. Descending the curvaceous stairs, the warm air hugs my toes as the mahogany floorboards creak in the golden heat like cicadas. As though moaning for a remedy. Perhaps a little mugwort will heal the wound? The deliquescent roses pull the house down, arching like a delicate, swollen shelter of lava; lymphatically, for hundreds of years. The perfume of them is so insatiable, it soaks the air. Foxes gather at the gate, whilst older women dressed in black believe it to be the sign of god and walk by whispering prayers and blessings for lost souls caught between heaven and earth. Khalëah sips splinters and willow bark from the glass. She felt a thick, meandering siege cramp up inside her, as her heart slithered away from her body and into the swimming pool of drowned insects. Its hands pull along the grass like a crocodile desperate for the water.

***

Back at the coffee shop, she drinks sombre bottled concoctions of belladonna and whiskey to commune with the perished in the daisies. The dogs howl at mountain wolves whilst a strange woman buries herself in the garden patch with growling vegetables and beetroot leaves that unfurl from her black hair.

Her bulbous, purple lungs wheeze in time within the heavy stomach of soil.

Her broom, pitch-fork ready to puncture demons and preserve their essence in bell-jars, and bake them into midnight blackberry pie. Under the rising seal-skin moon, sunflowers cut the sky with their teeth, drawing blood from the clouds like vampires and the slate walls cough up dark blue thistles; clay-heavy and Secret-scented.
I watched my reflection rebel against the beasts being born out of the water of the wishing well; spreading their bodies across the grass, over the violets to feast upon the doves in the dovecote. And a swarm of ants are summoned in the thunderstorm to honour dead honey bees with funeral bed rings of petals and martenitsas. That night I saw a fish that wasn't really a fish as much as she was a nymph, with stories on her tongue. Ghosts in her eyes and cigarette stained memories on her fingertips. Fireflies float about her; golden oracles carrying messages from the otherside. The honey-coloured days are left behind and a few passing trees blush scarlet, I see autumn's flame is ahead in this rotten fairytale that threatens to tear the moon like a cat butchering butterflies;

their paper wings, a collage stuck to the kitchen window. And she can't see...How everything she touches turns to ash. Her bitterness consumes her, the way a fig devours a wasp. Her violent, crayon brown eyes are scribbled with sorrow and transmit the sparks of sadness onto the shining rain; with a flick of her frown, she lights another cigarette, pulls out her liver and stabs it with shards of black mirror to divinate an answer...

She tells me:
"I don't know how to love. I've got nothing to offer, except my bones to make into chimes? My past haunts me too much to love you....*Čuckerdya pal m're per. Čáven save miseçe! Čuckerdya pal m're per. Den miseçeske drom odry prejiál!*"

Romani translation into English:
Ki shan i Romani Adoi san' i chov'hani— "Wherever gypsies go, there the witches are, we know."

Čuckerdya pal m're per, Čáven save miseçe! Čuckerdya pal m're pe Den miseçeske drom odry prejiál! —`Frogs in my belly, Devour what is bad! Frogs in my belly Show the evil the way out!"

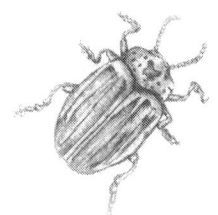

The Memory of Aphrodite- Poetic Hymn

"Muse tell me the deeds of golden Aphrodite Cyprian, who stirs up sweet passion in the gods and subdues the tribes of mortal men and birds that fly in air and all the many creatures that the dry land rears, and all the sea: all these love the deeds of rich-crowned Kythereia…
Hail, sweetly-winning, coy-eyed goddess! Grant that I may gain the victory and order you my song. And now I will remember you…"
Homeric Hymns 5 & 6 to Aphrodite (Greek epic C7th to 4th B.C.)

The sunrise opened apricot flesh,
golden juice bled over the water,
as the fragrance of the orchards in the zephyr,
ooze thick sweet scents of apples, jasmine and sea moss.
Startled by a sharp tang of lavender,
Upon the island of love and copper mountains.
Grace is a hard garnet thing.
Talk to me in poetry and sunsets on a swan's mute note.
She laughed like a deer,
Her pleasure sang the old worlds,
Melancholy eyes chasing after moths and butterflies,
Diamond tears in Cyprian seas.

Heavy with light and birds; of things in bloom,
Her wail hunts the dove,

Across the hatch of water,
Her voice hushed and rippling like the tide washing
   in a new day.
With a honeyed heartless, harlequin mouth,
bees emerged from their homes like a soul,
Leaving a body just to swarm around her,
A choir of droning devotion humming for her
   fair nimbus skin.

Lady of the mountains,
Of the temple that is heaven and earth,
Lady dawn, gold sandaled dawn.
Giantess planetary woman,
Of the shining eyes of night,
Lament in the house of muses,
All men shudder as they gaze at her sun
   dripped golden conch!
The foaming sea-men, hot lipped yet cowering
   with ecstasy,
Clutching at rising fruits in dreamy latitude,
Beguiling soft with curls and curves. Sucking
   plums and pomegranates.
She held the cosmos in her breasts,
She wore the sky in her hair,
stradling hotly full of peaches,
And they came at her knees.

Contradictory woman, complicated creature!
Curvaceous siren who fucked and loved in
   ceremonial exaltation!
Kingdom sparkle in her marguerite eyes.
She'll taunt you in reverie of poetry, wild horses and
   lemon groves,
She'll touch the place where that lost feeling was,
A touch so slight and swift as a butterfly's wing,
She is the flip of a coin between love and war,
Of star crossed lovers, sonnets and battles.
A tender smile on the blade lodged in a warrior's chest,
crowned in gold leaf and blood, broken hearts and bones.

That sweet dark is coming. The mystery of the
   water veiled one.
Like a sword slicing roses, keep a secret at least
   until morning,
The gorgeous miracle is her apocalyptic mouth,
Salt in the throat, salty sweetness!
Remember the heat as she rose from the sea,
Love, love is her season.
Don't turn away, don't hide your heart!
This is when the foam pulls you in,
The dolorous splash beckons you to the shore.

Persephone's Descent

A doorway groans open like a smoker's lung. stairs echo
with the sound of tapping, like hawkmoths battering
against a lightbulb or teeth chattering over tea cups.
Spiders lounging on dusty drain pipes like geisha. In
a room, a woman with hair curled like rope speaks in
a language that cascades from her mouth like incense
and old buildings. An urban fox rests on a garage island
like a pioneer for wild things, and a black cat murders
mice by the gutter, its poised body pouncing with fallen
arguments. hands in back pockets. A window screams
open, horrified at something that could be singing,
struggles in the spaces between concrete and monologues.
While a girl in denim and pigtails recites Christina
Rossetti's *'Goblin Market'* on the way home from school.
Pausing to photograph a dead pigeon with its heart
missing for her journal. In a crooked kitchen filled with
smiles, a couple slow dance to Americana, looking at each
other ardently, he's telling her sweet nothings to soothe
her. And the haunted child ties itself to the woman's
waist, floating like a death kite, growing in the quantum
realm. The quiet beauty of a muted TV and house plants
orbit the pain in her stomach. But she'll fix him a cup
of coffee. Outside, the fox with oil slick eyes stalks along
peeling fence palings, shouting fragments to grey skies
about poetry and oracles, bedroom silhouettes and the

sadness of a lost fallopian tube. Hearts breaking for a little love. She made the rain, that brutal baby, steeped in silver and blood. A voice chokes, ripples like a floodlight. *"You could never be a mother, who could ever love you."* The seaside town grief followed her to the city in a bitter salt breeze, it said she was destined to fail at raising flowers. The terrible edge of the tongue-sword in the soft living room glow punctures the womb. Tidy plump cushions stack like dolls, to hide the wretched shadow. One day she looked out into the clouds and her body rose up, out through the yawning window, taking the orchid and bedsheets with her. Even in sadness she displayed a regal bearing. The fox watched on, sitting on the roof of a red car. Staring into the stratospheric cool. The man walks the streets, heart hardened like coal, searching for dove feathers to build a flying contraption. He's trying to bring her back. He says; *Darling, I'll love you forever, let's go back to bed, I'll make you a chai, the darker the better, I'll kiss you gently, make your skin tingle, the softer the better. Come back to me in our summer brooding blue beach forever. Come back to me in our sugar kissed memory. Come back to me. Come back.*

Clear, Bright

Piercing pythia, Stark white and star bright,
Cinnamon girl, chanting lollipops, sugar in her teeth,
Summer stories pen and ink breathe, pretty blossom
   in the sunlight.

Briar roses tumble in the breeze, like satellites,
Thorns laid bare by the moonshine,
dripping cherry plum pie delight.

Full of golden dawn and strawberries and skin snow white,
Petals pressed between the glass,
Catching dandelions in the forest twilight.

Clair de lune soft blue of blue,
She's rather fanciful and subdued.
Trees that bloomed violet every September rain;
   Sail through.

A silvery laugh echo in the meadow rue of midnight,
Conversations with the garden, a remedy for belief,
and dreaming the aching bloom of yew, swishing in the fright.

The darkness lit by the rush of the blackbird's song,
Shared by her shy lustre as the frosted fruits fall,
In the vesper, pilgrim poppy prayers in the ground are gone.

A Quiet Crushing

Sixteen years and a day,
The spell was cast, my heart blistered.
Stinging, scalding. Scattered.
like broiling, boiling blood skies,
A heady broth of volcano-mouthed spite.

There is no way back from this.
The air is raw with screaming, hot shouts of rain,
An empty North Star brightness of loving you,
Clear- Appalling, a smudge of trembling cherry
   blond light,
You are cutthroat, trying to convince me of
  your prophecy.

In the whirring dissonance, I scratch your words
  off my soul.
Single breath of Plutonian rancour,
A language riddled with a very red, very
   wrong universe,
Rapture, rupture, repent.
I am not guilty of the storms.

I am a solar system of soothing, spiralled shells,
Fragile injury of faultline memories.
Ophelia shivered in the beaten earth, sonorous sorrow.

Sprung grace in the undertow, a soft note on a
   stretching song,
Kissing the chaos back into the image of a deer.

You knew exactly how to deliver hurt. Those Blue
   hail eyes.
I sang hymns and buried poppets to erase what you said,
This is the charm of the dog-star bursting,
Tideland breaking into the shape of you; a quiet crushing.
The immortal beauty of becoming maelstrom strangers.

A Letter to my Marigold

My Darling,
Looking back is like staring at fragments of a movie, flash pictures in variable sequences, images with no meaning to anyone but us; fragmented— a crush of doctors, a lagoon of agony— a cutting room narrative. I remember walking barefoot one day, with cardamom tea, writing poetry and listening to Lana Del Rey's song *Happiness is a Butterfly*. It was 10am on an early spring morning, a few months after surviving the ectopic pregnancy. I remember telling you that a clairvoyant once told me she saw a little death in my aura— our mouths smiled but our eyes spoke the language of grief. We knew what her prophecy now meant.

As months went by I wrote lists, scripts and scribbled prose; notes scattered across the coffee table, I'm trying to make sense of it all and erase the brutal memories that haunt me. I had no one to talk to, so I spoke to the paper. I desired dignity, I desired to regain control in my crumbled world and angry lunar rush. But mostly I yearned for connection. I was a listless wanderer orbiting my dance with death. I was so lonely wading through the tide of a thousand tomorrows, frothing through every horror— Yet people kept telling me to move on, you kept telling me to move on. I want to put my body into words. I want my severed fallopian tube in the sentences. The bloodstains in the paragraphs. I want our dying star on your tongue. Our story of pain, flesh-death and medical neglect. My horizon-eyed Lionheart, I want your story of almost losing me. I'm here! I'm really here, quite close to you! Singing a solitary hymn. I do not have the enormous strong heart of a humpback whale, I can not sing this alone, this aching is an obscure vast wilderness. But if we play catch and cast heartbreak between hands, we can share the weight of it and I will feel brave, no matter the wreckage.

With love,
Your Sweetheart

Beautiful Metamorphosis

Every night I die When I think of you,
Small beam and a heartbeat
with no name.
Wondering in the soft twilight,
If you're in the light.

River of red memories,
Hand on stomach,
No one is home.

Every day I live,
As you float away
And grow in a distant galaxy.
Astronomical grief,
Calm yet devastating,
But; it's quite beautiful…

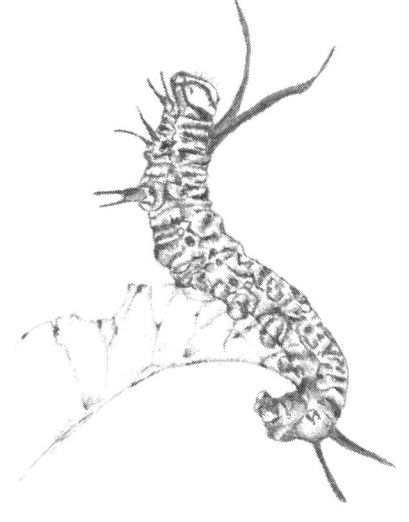

The Priestess of Black Pool

The Black Pool- an endless field of crushed queen
   of the night tulips,
In the beginning she speaks, the first glyph beaming,
Stood at the dangerous shore, loving the poppy
   in the reeds,
Cracking open secret bones and runes for the call.
Salt woman, Selkie Woman, seal-skin, soul-skin Woman,
Dark balsamic moon, Aphrodite fever dreamed woman.
She liked curved things, apples, peaches, the crest of a wave,
the shape of your heart.
She knows you are supposed to fall in love with her.

In this lagoon chapel a perfect damselfish,
shivering as if the night waters had surged her.
Eat her cockles slowly after a fresh dip in the lake,
In the shallows slipping, stretching with the dark waters,
Barracuda patterned and etched with ancient markings,
A wild creature, thrashing like a mako shark.

Deep tectonic plates heaved with her every movement
   in the lick of sunset,
Midnight brambled hair, tiger eyed and waning moon
   thoughts dripping on leaves,
Pouring herself everywhere but never quite fixed
   in one place.

With a mouth full of coral, she screeched a high
   wailing keening,
Like a sigil, like holy.
A gift of mayhem, dreams and moss velvet roots,
Of tendriled beasts beside her,
Beckoning you too close, you almost forget…

As the rain came down like thousands of pebbles crashing,
Secret smiles like fresh water pearls, held with love in the
   womb-shell.
She glistens with the moon.
At high tide, fish blow bubbles and she pulls you
   to the foam.

Voyage of soliloquy on the origins of the universe,
Dolphin sleek skin falters in the sudden cold unknown.
Particles in motion, her caressing ways are those of a
   treacherous animal,
Eaten alive by her riptide hunger, salt on tongue,
She's beautiful, that fish. A religious murky thing.
A siren of curses, promises and offerings.

Calico clam temple spilling at whose steps you
   collapse at the end of days,
Dark and light, light and dark- a bite of a woman!
Gills flush salinate and scarlet, the transfiguration
   of fish to flesh,

Webbed fingers reach up to crack open the
 ceiling of hearts,
A kiss of cobalt thunder, she'll drag you under!
Pray to the cormorants. Your river cannot survive
 her waters.
(Remember. Remember this, when you kneel before
 her abalone shell- your blood clots faster in the cold
 dark waters.)

Stranger Baby

Colliding comet,
Crashing into earth womb flesh,
Sail to Xibalba.

December rain,
A dying star enveloped in a galaxy of blood,
 Microcosm Macrocosm.

Ecliptic Ectopic,
Lonely gibbous ovary drifts in ghost tube,
Black hole orbits graveyard Uterus.

Sweet-dark astronaut,
Ammonite curled swimming up Orion's belt,
Armageddon butchered body.

Violent birth,
That was your attempt at dying,
A sacrificial life-giving voyage.

Cataclysmic asteroid,
There was a Virgo moon in my heart,
Stranger baby.

Hekate! (I keep your secrets well)

I asked the gods for a sign about you.
I was sworn to sacred mysteries, of the elysium,
Governess of the Eleusinian Mysteries,
(Promised to you unending secrecy, oh veiled one),
I talk to shadow and night and earth about you.
I sing to wind and wave and root about you.
I pray between trees and roads,
That's what I do.
(I keep your secrets well).

You know the way of dust, of the Deipnon.
You know the way the dream desert sands scorch my lips,
I know the spell of thirst,
You know my haunted eyes,
You know the way my body holds grief,
And the sadness coursing through my veins,
Like the river styx,
(You keep my secrets well).

My tongue was mute and I couldn't sing.
I thought the songbirds forgot about me,
But here I find a song about you,
Lodged inside my throat,
Pouring prayers in a bowl of ambrosia,
Torch bearer, light bringer!

I sing with fervent grace to you,
Nightingale longing and weaving thresholds,
You held my hand in ash and dust and dark,
Rose from ancient shadows, gentle flame!
(I keep your secrets well).

You gave the torch to me.
You told me life is a battlefield,
But grace is the portal.
It is the wayfinder in the shroud who walks with
   gentleness who knows me
You said;
(That poetry is our prophecy).
Born straddling death.
Pregnant birthing death.
You know my liminal rites of passage dear one.
(Please keep my secrets well).

You sent me on my way.
You told me life is a battlefield,
But grace is the portal,
(That dreaming is the doorway back into the gloaming).
I keep your secrets well,
I am your servant at the altar,
I am your student,
I keep your secrets well,
I keep your secrets well,
There is nobody else.

I will be waiting for you in my palace of grace

I will be waiting for you in my palace of grace and when the time is right you will know where to find me. Searching and longing and finding each other in every passing life. We found ourselves embedded in the atlas of clouds. Deserts, and rivers and minerals. Winds and civilisations of stone, the night of lapis lazuli and in the language woven with birds and jasmine. Dreams carved with ancestral psalms that could only be revealed by those who understood the creator's codex.

This is how the ancients speak to us, wings and stars and blue lotus flowers. Moon blood painted into clay. I found the one I first fell in love with again, whose freedom wasn't submerged in some distant direction but in the horizon of wild horses, floating in rivers, in poetry that found its way out of our tired thirsty mouths—-parched papyrus. My song of songs. Radiant, wild courageous heart I never gave up on you. Through the war and the waiting, I remembered you- battle scarred and humble. Pilgrim lover of the crescent moon. King of my heart. King of Cups. I am your shell in the reeds, glistening and cracked open for you. Like the love story of Isis and Osiris, I picked up the pieces of the body I once held on the sands and breathed into it in love. Even gods are romantics, so I offered roses of water, moringa and myrrh and gold to please them. So that they might bring us closer. My love, I will be waiting for you in my palace of grace. Together we will live forever. For love and death are the road to awe.

A Hymn of Love to the Earth

Hold out your hands and let me lay upon them a bunch
of freshly picked bluebells, delicate and brooding blue, like
teardrops cried by an ancient goddess who once walked
this terrain.

Find the fragrance of honey and jasmine seeping through
the holy scent of black earth after rainfall, breathe it all in
and you'll remember things you believed to be forgotten.

Look up into the deep bowl of celestial cerulean, drink
it up again and again, this is medicine for your eyes. Our
irises flicker in time with the fluidity of galaxies and the
flutter of comets.

Far out beyond the shoreline, you hear it. Beyond the
reach of any boat and on the foggy coastline scalloped by
shells and coves. Humpback whales, gentle giants of the
sea, chime their ancient prayers that hum like shamans
conjuring the rain.

Heat waves shiver across the grass like a black cat's purr,
the air is heavy and thunderstorm-yellow and ringing with
the whir of cicadas, a suspicious mantis praying for twilight
and fearful moths in search of the moon.

Take refuge in a shady grove where the grass is soft and cool underfoot, where the crickets sing and the sweet smell of ripe strawberries entice you like stout, scarlet sirens growing and coiling out of the damp ground.

They are a gift of erotic pleasure. Heart berries, indeed. *"Your role is to love me,"* they whisper as you ardently lick your red-stained fingertips.

I encourage you to drape your body over the earth, to be cradled by the gentle tickles of dew-soaked grass and buttercups. Allow your hair to be entangled with the dandelions as they dance to the rhythmic global breath.

Place your hands upon the wild, wild ground and feel the pitter-patter of a ladybird's feet upon your toes, whilst a honeybee rests on the warmth of your breast in the rudimentary setting sun.

Reach your fingertips out towards the remote, swollen sky to feel the fresh breeze kiss your wrists as your palms sway with the wide threshold of heavy clouds.

Kneel for the soulful, sparkle of all the stars. They are but throbs of one body harmonised by a primitive pulse beating to the roaming of your blood.

Lounge by a quilt of moss unfurling upon the cottony edge of a pond, and be mesmerised by golden apples gliding along its surface, like globes of light weaving through eventide.

Run into the fray of falling foliage and sweetgrass as they float onto the mud.

Feel the fever dream of the moon swishing over mountains like a ball of silk as you sit by the river to watch its reflection glow like worlds within worlds
within worlds.

Hear the rippling language of the waters talk to the warrior trees as they stretch out in silent prayer. Make love in the rain, under the protective bows of a weeping willow. Skin upon skin, lips caressing lips in the here and now, shrouded by the endless undulating orbit of ferns.

Look deep into the amorous eyes of your lover as you sweep their hair back from their ears, and truly see the wilderness bursting from their eyes in the gloaming.

Like the freedom cry of a falcon, the laughter of an otter, the sweetness of a faun and the mystery of a fox all bundled up into a human being you are unafraid to love. And they return their love for you, in all your storms and in all your grit.

Open yourself up to the voices of silver bells, the rush of waterfalls, the little robin song and the silence of mosses, and you will be humbled.

Oak and blackberries, sea grass and cockle shells, stag beetles and the winter wren. The whole world is woven together like a wild basket, and it is big enough to hold us too.

We are reminded every day that nature is magic coming to life.

The heart of a blue whale is as big as a house, with chambers tall enough for a human being to stand in. A fig is born when a female wasp lays her eggs inside a flower, after which she dies and decomposes. The fruit is evidence of her soul's transformation, evidence of reincarnation.

Breathing in the scent of mother earth releases the hormone oxytocin, a chemical that promotes bonding. We are held in the loving arms of Gaia, it is therefore no wonder we sing whilst gardening or walking in the woods. A giant flock of starlings in the sky is called a murmuration. Thousands of birds becoming one huge spirit bird! It is a sea of birds swimming with the clouds and blocking out the sun, gliding together like shooting stars dancing in the afternoon haze.

Sometimes the magic is so bright, our mind cannot fathom it. Sometimes the truth that we are all connected is so vast, nobody believes it.

I am a bird made of birds, I have countless wings that hum and soar the depths of my dreams.

I am a raging ocean with a heart as big as a blue whale's, and you can stand up in its chambers, where my love will carry you. I carry you in my heart for I have so much space.

I am the soil holding out my arms to you whilst singing with devotion. I am dying inside many flowers, over many lifetimes, and I offer you my fruit, I offer you all that I am. This is what I was born to do. To live, to fly, to love, to die, to live again!

I take great pleasure in roving in the sweet brutality of life and of the earth. I marvel at such feral divinity that weaves through each creature and each plant like a spider's tender web.

This is a hymn of love to the earth,

We are all wildflowers in this meadow called life,

Our hearts belong with the roses, the poppy and the plum.

Rebecca's Requiescat—
I Dream That You Forgive Me and My Body Turns To Water
Short Story-Poetic Prose

13.
The mangroves are flooded. They catch Gobies, Grunts, and Grey snappers in great nets torn open, gutted. Spilling onto the deck like giant teardrops, silver orbs of gasping fish. Scales reddened by the scarlet lustre of stab wounded clouds. Rivergod tears pouring onto boats, crying at the cruelty of man. Mangrove Jack mouths 'pop pop *popping*' as though trying to mutter their final prayers. Gills burning like cigarettes in the cough of November's dry dawn. A thousand eyes startled. Death-wild. Pleading. A frenzied wriggling to hold each other in their final cold, choking minutes. I envy them in their brotherhood but I still laugh at their pitiful attempt to hug one another with the slip of fragile fins.

One by one, the fishermen reach into the buckets, scoop them out, slap them down, and slit them throat to tail. On their dying day, they die alone anyway, just like the rest of us. I walk on toward the cove where the glass bottle choir whistles in the breeze, Delaney scuttles along the rock pools hunting for shells and sea glass, her cherub face haloed by refracted sunlight shorelines.

A hundred years ago they found the body of a young woman face down in the water and gnarled between Ceriops roots like a caged mermaid, flesh like wet paper, hair like bleached seaweed and with a large crescent moon mark on her throat. Stories now weave around these parts of water horses appearing on the river bed during the slit moon, beguiling and dove-grey. Dragging people into the river with a low silky moan. At least this is what they teach the kids, scaring them not to swim in the river at night. Some say they can hear moans and lyrical words during the flooding months, as though the water is reaching for them, calling them in.

It is believed the river kelpies had been people once, grown out of their skins, giving up their bodies. Kelpies that carry the dead souls inside them. Kelpies that whistle and moan, calling the chosen into the gloaming. People tell all kinds of stories to try and make sense of grief.

A fisherman stands along the shore. Wellies grounded. Fishing line flying. "Day for it! Caught a whopper! She's a beauty!" he smiles. Holding up the snapper ensnared by the hook like a witch tied to a noose. I double take and swear I see the fish peer at me vacantly. Her parched lips strangled to mutter something.

Breathless she whispers, "It is time."

12.
I imagined it. I say to myself, standing by the bathroom sink. *I'm seeing things, the doctor said it's all part of it. I forgot to take Olanzapine this morning because Delaney couldn't find her shoes and we ran out of milk.* I was preoccupied. These last days, my mind is a colourless frontier. My sea-blue eyes sunken. They stare back at me in the mirror the same way that fish stared at me. Knowing? A cry for help? The drugs are drying out my skin, becoming arid grey mottled patches; my voice is hoarse and I'm always thirsty. This damned heatwave scalds my cracked eyelids.

There's a town parade this afternoon. I consider stepping out to take in the festivities but I'm not a Calliope sugar-sweet woman, the vibe is not for me. Delaney is asleep anyway.

There's water trickling down the living room wall, I better call the plumber, there are electrical wirings and plugs behind the plaster and framing. Could be dangerous.

11.
There's nothing much to eat but I make a cup of tea whilst Delaney sits on my lap. Her body is a heavy devotion and her golden curls smell like chamomile. I take in one last breath and it hurts and I feel tender at the sight of her tearing at the shell bracelet on her wrist.

Her hands then reach out and wrap around my neck like rope. The plumber came and went, told me there's no water leakage, that the wall isn't even wet, that I wasted his time. I said, "I know what I saw, the heatwave dried it up." The weather report says thunderstorms are on the forecast. I can feel the shift in the air as I turn all the lights on and wash the dishes. There is a list of things I must put in order first. My days are slinking out like eels, this house is sullen, sick as a heart, and haemorrhaging light.

Thunder claps. Startles me from a dream of a thousand eyes and a thousand roots in a dark arc. Sweat slips down my skin, patting hair to my face. My mouth is still so thirsty. I catch a glimpse of Delany in salmon red rain boots splashing in the marshy garden. When the creek floods, the water sometimes reaches the houses, pooling around ankles and cabinets like mottled silver, resting between toes, quiet as butterflies.

Lifting my shirt to take a shower, I see my spine, a heavy ridge along my back, hair dripping like sweaty seaweed. My eyes are haunted, goldfish frantic. Glazed. I have no eyebrows and my skin itches as it sheds like pencil shavings. *Look at the state of me, who could ever love me? God, I'm really just alone, I'm so alone!* Crouching in the bath crying, curled like a shell I hear distant laughter in the lightning. The drugs ate my beauty like maggots eating dead fruits.

The wall bleeds water again and there's now a mould patch growing over the ceiling. I better call that fucking plumber again.

10.
The house feels hook tight. Water is slowly trickling in, closing in. Streams along the windows, puddles soaking shoes. A minnow slips through the mouldy crack, scuffing the wall and plops down, flopping on the tiles next to the door frame. I see Delaney by the garden fence posts like a little fish wriggling near shark teeth. Going over to examine the peculiarity of the minnow, I see thin films of pearly webbing growing between my fingers, growing past the knuckles and thickening. Panic-stricken I begin to chew and pick at this in-between flesh ferociously but it keeps growing back.

The minnow stares and 'pop pops' its mouth rapidly. *It is time.* I hear that voice again.

I do not want to talk to the voices anymore or see these things, I am frightened. I want it all to stop. Get out of my blood, get out of my head. A fact dressed up in melodramatic melancholy. I try to sleep again to rest my mind from the haunted things.

9.

The yearly river flood vomits out into the sea and brings with it a great cull. There are more hooks than fish in the harbour. Men teaching lads how to fish like a rite of passage, girls wading in the waters in pretty dresses like prayers. Fish festivities forget the dangers. It is the drowning season. I left the washing up in piles in the sink but I put the laundry on and went out to the promenade, to the markets. I give permission for my thoughts to wonder as Delaney trundles alongside me, her little hand squeezing mine with so many smiles poking through ringlets. She's sweeter than a lollipop; my little sugarfish.

I think about that time I looked up the meaning of my name. Rebecca, from the Hebrew word *Rivqah*. Means snare, tie, bind, noose. That's about right. Most days I feel like I'm choking. Hanging on with harsh breath. I'm drowning in the air.

"Mummy! That big cloud reminds me of the cloud we saw on the beach, that time we made ourselves sand mermaids!"

And for a moment I want my ribs to carve open with love and I want it to kill me instantly.

8.

We arrived at *Sea Salt Fishmongers* on the harbour. The air tastes like 'catch of the day' and salt and vinegar with the rattle of smiling strangers exposing fangs. Josh, my jolly sailor bold, stands behind the counter with a smile as warm as the September sun. This is the business that we built together, not far from where I proposed to him. He's been up since the crack of dawn, putting cart loads of aquatic carcasses on ice. Prawns, oysters, squid, salmon, and more. Some are already hooked, gutted, and skewered. The spokes of the fan on the ceiling look like long knives cutting through the daylight, its shadow casting blades across customers' throats. Fish on display grin back at me with pouty requiescat.

I see the dark haired woman sitting at a table again. She writes poetry then hits the beach in her sexy summer dresses. She comes in here often and not for the fish. Her October olive eyes have an oceanic pull. Without uttering a sound she reels men towards her like caught fish, a beckoning creature in a saucy orbit. Her presence hushes people like a waterfall. She's not from around here—displaced like a wrong deity. I hate her as much as I hate myself yet she was everything I wished I could be, something darling and free with a messy heart that everyone falls in love with, an exotic contradiction of British bubble gum naivety and flecks of something primal, a sultry huntress. Lana del Rey's *Summertime Sadness* chimes in the background, poignant and prophetic. I casually think that could be my funerary song perhaps?

Josh takes one look at my hands, the dried blood now scabbing over between my fingers. Horrified, he asks, "Sunshine, why do you do this to yourself?" I say, "I'm fine, you know I pick my skin when I'm anxious."

I stare at Josh and think *it's times like this when the marine haze lifts off the sea that I realise there are things you still don't know about me. Like sometimes I'm afraid my sadness is too deep and that one day you might have to help me navigate it or cast me away. I try to keep my eyes level to the horizon and beyond, in our boat with fin and little fish, just off the coast of Korora bay, listening to Summertime Sadness by Lana del Rey.*

7.
Outside we pass by seagulls stalking tourists and head up to Muttonbird island. Birds rain across the grey swell. In the distance, I hear horses where the waves crash up against the old lighthouse. The sky is yawning open. This close to the wild things I feel completely free, but I can feel the pull of it in every cell of my body. It is a deep, sorrowful, yearning feeling. To jump. Out here I'm as calm as eagles. I try to eat my words. I eat my errors. I am only a guest here. A fleeting tempest.

6.
The dark shift darkens. The ground heaves and sighs into wet sands like the mandible of a great whale and proteas in bright profusion scream at the sky. An opal of thunder cracks in labradorite clouds. The sea argues with the river and then rises up like an octopus. Flying fish emerge from the waves like a soul leaving the body. Rain clouds opened up like an ancient womb, birthing emotions I cannot. Salt water. Salt tears. And a shower of marine life falls on Muttonbird island like bullets.

Dashing for cover under a lone tree we are curtained by falling sky fish! Mackerel, tuna, cod, guppies, eels, pike, blue tangs, haddock, and more. Delaney laughs and claps. I wait by the crusted rocks, watching the flesh slide off the cliff, some plop back into the sea, others snap to the ground. One fish comes cresting up, its narrow belly flopping over the slick moss. Its marble eyes curse me and I fall to the ground, pulling out bad memories as though pulling out innards.

On the frothing shore, crescent moon hoof prints trail out from the water, up the coastline, and dot across the riverbed. My lips are cold and chapped so we head home and I pretend none of this happened, it's all in my head like most things. It's time to take my next dosage of Olanzapine.

5.

It is a growl of a night, a bestial hurt. My malaise soaks through marrow deep. I make pumpkin soup in a daze, burn the fish pie, and undercook the potatoes. Delaney does not notice. Josh will be home soon and he will anchor me. My skin is thirsty and peeling so I run a bath. Underneath the peeling flakes now trailing over my body, there's a layer of sleek skin, mottled and silky tight like a porpoise. My hair is now cold, white. I am glistening. Swampy. Accepting that this is the way it is.

In the bath, my skin appears to shimmer like opals and I dream in red and rope. The house churns, becomes heavy and bulbous, squeezes itself like a sponge, arching eel-like and making arresting sounds to push me out. Keyholes leak tiny streams of water and wrap around my hands like a best friend pulling me to a happy place.

That night I dream of those fish in the rain clouds, falling onto hooks and hanging by the river. I feel a sudden weight on my chest. Something wet. There is a creature keening on the bed. I hold my breath. Then it is gone. Holding my hands up to the moonlight I find large slick bite marks set into my wrists like a stamp of approval. Josh cuddles into me and asks, "Is everything alright?" I say "Everything is alright."

4.
Scarlet morning scratches my eyes. I wake up to the sound of the pied butcher bird invoking a new day. I think about that parade the day before, celebrating life-giving sustenance with dead fish to feed us and drowned victims that were called to the waters. Fish on land. Bodies in the mangroves. The irony happens every year. I still feel dehydrated, choking in this humid air but my body, now barnacled, streams water down my curves and pools at my feet. Cockles and conch shells fall out of my hair like lice.

3.
Riverbank sermons sing to me. I am in a thirsty atmosphere. I accept it with grace and release the deep pressure behind my stinging eyes. I feel my soul moving out of my fingertips, I am becoming something else and I am calm. I laugh and think I could be happy inside a horse. I hear a wailing and intoning language in the breeze. I do not understand it, but I know it, and I want to follow it.

2.
On this last day, I put everything in order. Send Delaney to her father. Iron your shirts. Wash the dishes. Feed Fin. Plump up the cushions. Hang the laundry. Pull down the photos from the fridge. Mop the floor. I write you a

letter. Leave it by your fish bone art. I leave quietly. Walk past the long body of the coast. I am disorientated and nobody is coming for me. I think about how you will find me—find the house empty. Would you come for me?

I'm almost there, past the point of no return. It is time.

For a moment I stop to uproot a protea. Dig your own grave, I told myself. Because no one else will. But every time I see your face and you asked if I was okay, I thought Help me! But I always felt I couldn't. Wouldn't. Like if you flicked the searchlight into my eyes you still wouldn't find the answers as to why I felt this way and why I did what I did. I see your knees buckle with grief.

1.
In the dark, their echoing curses boom like the crash of waves. My sadness dissipates with the rain. Everything sounds clear, so true, porous bright blue. Pulling my socks off, I stand serenely balanced between roots and water. The river is lunar. My body levitates before the fall. Breath potent between gasping heartbeats. A large branch snaps. I lose sight all the way down until it is dark enough to feel the thousand eyes and the thousand roots waiting for me. A motion of something brushing and binding my legs together as a light lulled to me.

I'm whistling with the tide, calling to you from the deep. Roaming wild and free in the herd of white waves. I'll come back to you with the floods. I'll sing to you under the slit moon. My ruins rise with the waters, each one the sound of stones drifting away to make me whole.

My heart was a very fragile thing and I had nothing left to give, I couldn't fight what was in my nature. I had to break away from my namesake, from myself and leave my Ophelia-body with the groves. I tried so often to grip the edge of goodness. To be a good daughter, a good mother, a good lover, a good friend . . . I didn't feel enough. I didn't feel good enough. Just projecting something into empty air.

I was brave wasn't I? It wouldn't have been easier if I had stayed. I had to rove. I felt my throat separate from my body and vanish into the tide, and I smiled and smiled into the wild, and promised that . . . after all this, after all this . . . I love you still. I am now the beauty of the after. The beautiful pilgrim of the river. I am the forever kelpie. I dream that you forgive me and my body turns to water.

***

In dedication to Rebecca. Goodnight sweet Kelpie, may your soul finally roam free in cosmic oceans.
30°17'48" S 153°08'22" E

My dear friend Rebecca was diagnosed and struggled with psychotic depression. She took her own life weeks before her 30th birthday in November 2021. She was a quirky, free-spirited Sagitarius who loved living by the river and the sea in Coffs Harbour, Australia. Since Sagittarius is half horse, I had her, in death, transform into a water horse. Setting her free in her favourite place. Whilst Kelpies are from Scottish folklore, water horses are also associated with Poseidon and I imagine her immortalised roving free with the waves in his oceans and with other water spirits.

This is a collection of poems and prose that have featured in an array of literary journals and anthologies throughout the year of 2021 during Katie's recovery from surviving her ectopic pregnancy. Katie wished to bring them all together in one place with the inclusion of 6 poems newly published in this chapbook.

Acknowledgement

The Priestess with the Poppy Heart, Honeysuckle Summers & Stranger Baby first published with **Poetry Undressed**

Luna Moth, December Dawn & Insignificant first published in **The C Word Mag**

A Hymn of Love to the Earth first published in **Rebelle Society**

Persephone's Descent first published with **Hecate's 'Decay' Anthology**

When the Roses pulled the house down first published in **Hecate's 'Birth' Anthology**

The Oracle & Sura's Fox first published with **Wandering Autumn Magazine**

The Priestess of Perdition first published with **Pressure Cooker Literary**

Rebecca's Requiescat first published with **Mulberry Literary** online, and then in print with **Little Lion Press Anthology: Death & Desire**

A Quiet Crushing first published in **Empyrean Literary Anthology**

A Letter to my Marigolde first published in **Marigolde Press Anthology: Wildling & Sprout**

Beautiful Metamorphosis first published in **Beyond the Veil Press 'Tea with my Monsters' Anthology**

Photographs

The Priestess of Perdition: Wendy Rivara-Self portrait
The Snow Priestess: Sarah Cook by Lily Moss
The Memory of Aphrodite: Despina Chrysanthou- Self Portrait
The Priestess of Black Pool: Katie Ness by Keith Craig

This collection is dedicated to Despina, my Cypriot muse, my Aphrodite sister.

Eise toso omorfi oso ena xrisafenio livadi, me mia kardia toso megali kai fotini san ton ourano. Se evxaristw gia ti filia sou.

You are as beautiful as a golden meadow, with a heart as big and bright as a blue sky, thank you for your friendship.

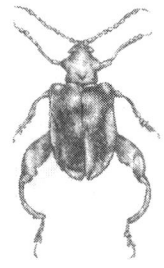

Thank you

Thank you Phil for always reminding me to be your 'big brave girl', thank you for being my mentor, my yoda, my septic peg…You are very much missed, goodnight and fly far with the goldfinches.

Thank you to my dear friend 'Old Man' Mark Whittacker for giving me a gentle nudge to publish my poetry and for believing in me.

Thank you to Isabelle, Editor of *Poetry Undressed* for being the first literary platform to publish my poetry, after over 50 rejections elsewhere I almost gave up.

Wendy darling my witchy soul sister across the pond. Thank you for tuning into my heart and helping me navigate the weather of my moods better than I do.

Claire, thank you for your wisdom and detailed eye for beauty, you are my voice of reason, your constructive criticism (and hilarious blunt humour) is very much appreciated!

Despina my Cypriot muse and poetess who inspired this collection, you continue to inspire me with your passion and talent in the arts-from theatre to dance to poetry, is there nothing you can not do? You are the 11th muse!

Sarah, your patience and sweetness brought a sense of calm in my otherwise tumble jumble writer's mind.

Sharada, my Saraswati sister and teacher. Thank you for all you taught me on the Be Woman Project and for helping me activate and realise my own Saraswati nature.

Janie, thank you for the dreamy memories and meandering thoughts every sunrise in Bali. I felt so free and beautiful around you.

Hazel. Thank you for the giggles and barefoot 'Dirty Girls!' muddy puddle rain dancing, it helped me get out of my writer's sulky funk.

To my beloved Craig, my warrior that protects my heart, thank you for believing in me and listening to me twitter on reciting my work out to you at stupid O'clock and providing me with copious mugs of tea.

To Nanna Monica, who instilled in me a love of reading and stories, I live for you, everything I do is always for you, you are my constant to remind me to always be loving, forgiving and kind, I hope I make you proud? Every day I miss you, I hope you found the spirit of my baby and you're looking after her up there.

To all the priestesses I have known/will know/know- keep on weaving, seeking and dreaming

Katie Ness is a freelance writer in the UK. She has articles, essays & poetry published with a variety of literary sites, anthologies and print magazines such as *Kindred Spirit, Femme Occulte, Witches Magazine, Occulture, Hecate Magazine, Beyond the Veil Press, The C Word Mag, Mulberry Literary* and more.

She has an Honours degree in Fine Art and is currently studying diplomas on the history of Ritual & Magic, Celtic Mythology and Archeology of the British Isles. Her MA is forthcoming.

When not writing Katie is a yoga & wellness teacher specialising in women's health and feminine spirituality, Ayurvedic Hatha yoga & Yoga Nidra, women's circles, Cacao Ceremonies and more.

In her free time she can be found roaming across Britain and overseas to seek out the sacred feminine and occult sites in the landscape.

She is presently crafting a second poetry book and travel memoir over copious amounts of tea.

Katie is a practising hedgewitch and priestess who works with goddesses, ancestors and the spirit world.

Follow her on Instagram *@katie_wild_witch*

These poems are rituals, taking the form of fragmented psalms, dreams, letters and even prayers for the primordial storm of the wild feminine.

Katie explores the liminal space between the body of the earth as a primal entity in relation to the body as self in nature. Eco-poetry meets erotic and melancholic magical realism. Her words pour out speculative lyricism into a reimagining of ancient hymns as though channelled by Sappho herself. Attempting to retrieve a silenced female voice from the depth of the earth, invoking Aphrodite and other immortals.

Katie's poems and short story dwell within the tender, shifting borderland between language, and between poetic forms, to examine the shape and texture of memories, of love, time, dreams and what it is to be a woman. Abundant with multiplicities, these poems dance with lush dreamy eroticism or despair, executed with painterly strokes of the wild complex geography of the ancient feminine coursing through our earth and women's hearts today.

Printed in Poland
by Amazon Fulfillment
Poland Sp. z o.o., Wrocław

31295467R00047